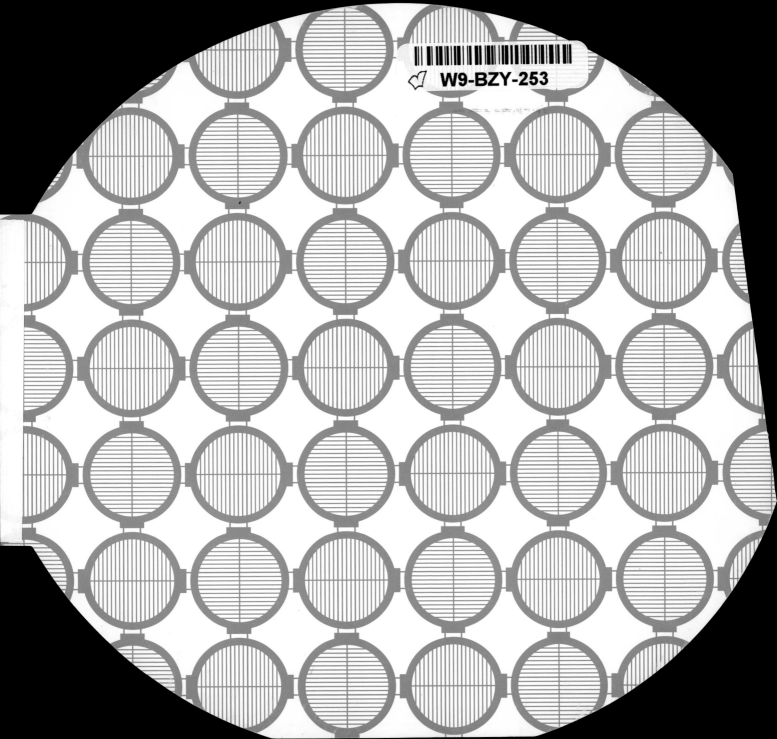
W9-BZY-253

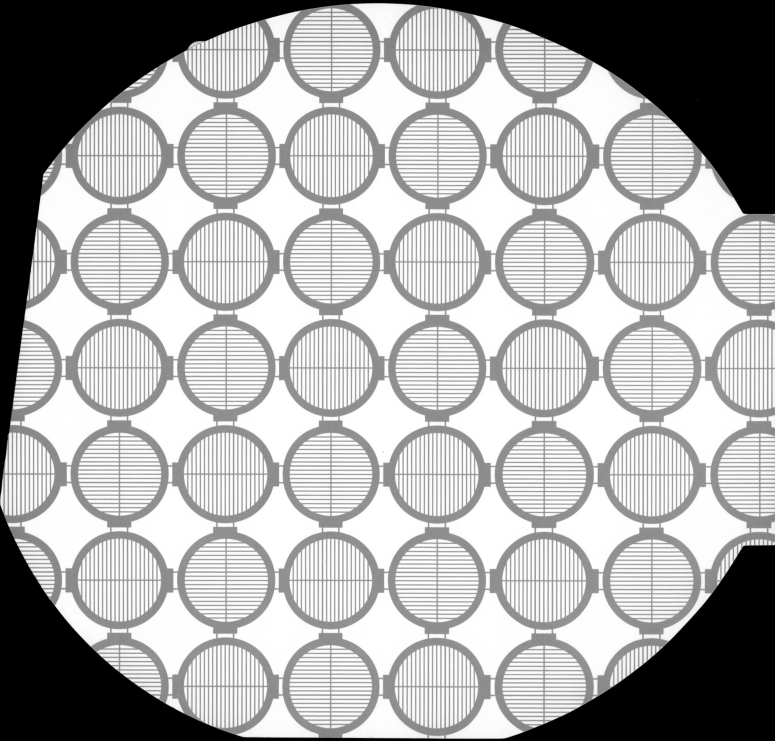

BARBECUE

50 Easy Recipes

ACADEMIA
BARILLA

EDITED BY

ACADEMIA BARILLA

PHOTOGRAPHY BY

ALBERTO ROSSI
CHEF MARIO STROLLO
CHEF LUCA ZANGA

RECIPES BY

CHEF MARIO GRAZIA

TEXT BY

MARIAGRAZIA VILLA

GRAPHIC DESIGN

MARINELLA DEBERNARDI

EDITORIAL COORDINATION ACADEMIA BARILLA

CHATO MORANDI
ILARIA ROSSI
LEANNE KOSINSKI

CONTENTS

THE BEAUTY OF GOING... OUT OF THE FRYING PAN AND INTO THE FIRE

"On fiery logs the roast turns on its spit and crackles"
Giosuè Carducci, *San Martino*, in *Rime Nuove*, 1887

What could be more relaxing than eating outside, on the porch or in the garden, on a balmy night in late spring or early summer? The darkness falls and the barbecue coals glow red. The mouth-watering scent of the grill fills the air like a smile. Sipping a glass of good wine or a cold beer, you can enjoy a foretaste of the pleasures to come: a juicy T-bone steak, a delicious grilled salmon, an inviting slice of grilled polenta with Gorgonzola... Meanwhile, your friends arrive in dribs and drabs, in a crescendo of chattering, laughter and exchanged confidences. Because a barbecue is not only a more informal way of cooking and enjoying food; it is the most convivial way possible of sharing a special moment with others.

The age-old adventure of open fire cooking
Grilling and cooking on a spit, exploiting the heat of the coals, is one of the oldest and simplest methods of cooking known. Ever wonder how far back barbecuing dates? According to the most recent archaeological finds, man is thought to have learned to use fire in a controlled manner about a million years ago (and unintentionally, even earlier). Cooking is the first element of culture in human history, involving the transformation of food found in nature through the use of heat, and making all foods that would be harmful if were consumed raw, edible. Moreover, it enables us to smoke food, which preserves it for longer.
In essence, open fire cooking, which enhances the flavor of any food, has not changed much over time, although it has clearly evolved in terms of

the tools, methods, tricks and techniques used. It has maintained a special significance, compared to cooking indoors, and features in the religious festivities, festivals, food gatherings and cultural life of almost all parts of the world.

The origins of the word "barbecue" are uncertain. Some believe it derives from the Haitian term *barbacoa*, imported by the Spaniards in the sixteenth century at the time of the discovery and colonization of the American continent. The term refers to a "bed of twigs" fastened on logs, on which meat was smoked over hot coals. For others, the word derives from a contraction of the expression *de la barbe à la queue*, meaning "from beard to tail", which the French used in the sixteenth century to refer to the process of cooking a whole animal on the spit, practiced by the Indians of the New World. The word "barbecue" later entered the English vocabulary to indicate both the equipment on which meat is cooked outdoors, and the food cooked on an open fire on those occasions when friends and family gather to lunch or dine together around the warm glow of the coals.

It's easy to say barbecue

There are different types of barbecue: some are fixed (made of masonry), some mobile (on wheels) and some portable (of smaller dimensions). They can be fueled by charcoal or wood, gas or electricity, and even solar energy in environmentally friendly versions. They can have iron, cast iron or stainless steel grates, as well as countless accessories and sometimes even a cover. Before buying one, it is important to decide what type of equipment best suits your needs, especially given the space available (a rooftop terrace is not exactly the gardens at Versailles...).

Whatever model you chose, your barbecue should be stable and as high as a table, so as not to have to bend down while cooking. It should come with a base into which the ashes can drop, ventilation holes (adjustable would be a plus) and a movable, height-adjustable grate, enabling you to regulate the heat intensity by lowering or lifting the food from the coals. Although the best results are achieved *en plein air*, it is possible to grill food all year round on indoor barbecues or in the beloved old fireplace. Imagine a cold winter night, with a snowstorm raging outside, and the aroma of a chicken cooking on the spit over a roaring fire rising from the fireplace. What could be cozier, especially in the company of friends and family?

Little smoke and lots of fire

The oldest and most primitive way of cooking is to place food directly on the hot coals. This gives it a special aromatic complexity, and is suitable mainly for vegetables, which are served after carefully removing any charred parts.

Grilling, instead, is a form of cooking that can be either direct, placing the food for a few minutes on a grate placed above a layer of coals, or indirect. In the case of direct cooking, food cooks by means of the radiation generated by the coals, the convection of hot air rising from the brazier, and the conduction of the red-hot grill. It is not just the high temperature (over 750 °F, or 400 °C) that gives the food that characteristic "grill scent" that cannot be replicated in the kitchen; it is also the spilled liquids that, evaporating on the hot charcoals, rise again in the form of aromatic smoke. This can provide a sour, pungent taste, and must be carefully controlled so as not to cover the food's intrinsic flavor. Similarly, it is important to control flare-ups that can occur while cooking due to the burning of fats: smoke and flare-ups form harmful substances that should be limited through an efficient management of the cooking process and the use of proper implements. When performed correctly, grilled food is not only rich in aromas and flavors, but it is also healthy as it reduces the need for additional dressings and eliminates excess fat.

Indirect grilling is similar to oven-baking, and is suitable for longer cooking times and lower temperatures (270-390 °F, or 130-200 °C), such as when preparing roasts, poultry or fish. It exploits the movements of convection currents generated inside a closed chamber, in which the heat emanates from the opposite side to that in which the food is placed.

When grilling, cooking times are always approximate. There are so many variables at play – food thickness, charcoal temperature, distance from the heat source – that the timing can never be guaranteed. But, after all, the beauty of barbecuing is that it unites reason and feeling: although an exact science in some respects, requiring a careful eye not to burn the food, in other respects it leaves plenty of room for individuality.

The ABC of grilling

Good quality charcoal is the easiest fuel to use. It must be produced from fine woods, because, in a barbecue, the aromatic smoke it generates impermeates the meal. Make sure the charcoal is dry and place it in a pyramid on a base of crumpled sheets of newspaper and small pieces of very dry wood. Pour on some alcohol and wait a few minutes, then light a fire with a long match. As soon as the charcoal begins to burn, stoke it up and allow some air to circulate with a fan or with bellows. Then, with a poker, scatter the charcoal over the entire surface of the brazier. When the flames are completely extinguished and the charcoal begins its slow combustion process, place the grate on the brazier, about 4-6 in. (10-15 cm) above the charcoal, and let it become red hot. When a thin layer of white ash forms on the surface, you can start cooking.

There are various kinds of scented wood that, when used for grilling suitable foods, can add flavor and aromas to the dishes. Plants that grow along the sea and are permeated with the smell of salt, such as maritime pine, tamarisk or red juniper, are ideal for cooking sea fish. For red meats, it is best to use perfumed essences, such as cedar, larch, cherry or various types of fir. To give flavor to white meats, instead, English oak, mastic and the entire oak family are the perfect choice. The *gourmet griller* should use olive wood for lamb and pear wood for veal.

Whatever fuel you choose, the virtue that must never be lacking is patience. The fact of not having a precise dining time and of enjoying the courses at random, as and when they are ready (if one were to wait until they're all ready, they would become cold and less flavorsome), contribute to making the barbecue atmosphere even more pleasant and relaxed.

The griller's tools
Using the right accessories can make your barbecue a breeze. To protect yourself from the fire, it is important to use fireproof pot holders and gloves (preferably long, so as to cover and protect the forearm) and, optionally, a classic apron (which looks the part, no doubt about it). The griller then needs a series of magic barbecuing wands: tongs, spatulas, forks, spoons and brushes, all with longer handles than those of the cutlery normally used in the kitchen.

For meat, particularly useful are a probe thermometer to determine the

cooking temperature, a sharp knife and fork for slicing, and a grooved cutting board to collect the juices. Folding grates are also useful, enabling you to turn food easily and carefully, as are long skewers with an insulating handle, enabling you to turn them without burning your hands. Wooden skewers need to be soaked in water for 30 minutes before using to keep them from burning; if marinade is needed, you can marinate the meat while the skewers soak, then skewer the meat cubes and cook them right away. Finally, a drip tray is essential to prevent fats dripping on the fire from roasts or game cooked on the spit; this avoid sparks, spattering and bad smells. Grillers may also find a fan or bellows useful to blow the fire. A good safety tip is to keep a fire extinguisher nearby, in case of accidentally starting a fire.

The art of marinating
While waiting to be grilled, food can be rubbed, from a few minutes to a few hours before, with a mixture of spices to enhance the flavor and form a tasty and crispy crust while cooking. Since grilling does not make use of liquids, food is often marinated, that is, immersed for at least half an hour in a marinade for the purpose of softening and flavoring it. Although recipes generally explain whether and how to marinate the ingredients, there is never just one marinade possible, but countless variations on the theme. In principle, marinades, used in Italian cooking since the Renaissance, are an emulsion in which to steep the food to be grilled. They comprise a fat component, such as oil or butter, and an acidic or alcoholic substance, such as yogurt, vinegar, wine or spirits, with the addition of spices and herbs. Naturally, marinades are effective on the surface and not in depth, and so it is good practice to marinate food in small pieces, so that they are better

flavored and softened. Moreover, frozen meat should never be marinated. Before marinating meat or fish, remove any waste parts and excess fat, then rub on the marinade ingredients evenly and leave them to rest in the refrigerator in a closed container (preferably not metal) to prevent bacterial proliferation. Once the marinating time indicated in the recipe is up, thoroughly drain off the marinade before cooking and let meat rest at room temperature before grilling. Marinades may also be used to baste meat or fish while cooking, but not when these are already cooked, because the marinades may contain residual bacteria. For this same reason, marinade that has had raw meat or fish in it shouldn't be used for brushing: you can reserve some of it before adding the meat or the fish, then use the reserved marinade for brushing when cooking.

Here are some basic marinades, the proportions of which are left entirely up to you. For fish and shellfish: lemon or lime juice, olive oil, garlic, parsley, thyme, salt and white pepper, and ginger for an exotic note. For white meat: olive oil, lemon juice or white wine or white vinegar or balsamic vinegar or beer, sage, rosemary, salt and black pepper. For red meat: garlic and rosemary, pepper, salt and red wine (optional). For game: garlic and rosemary, pepper, salt, cinnamon, cloves and juniper berries. For vegetables: olive oil, lemon juice, oregano, thyme, salt and pepper. For fruit: the fruit's juice, brown sugar, spirits, fresh mint and anise. Marinades are not used with cheese.

The tricks for a perfect barbecue
Here's how to prepare the perfect, memorable barbecue.
First of all, always use the finest ingredients and cook them with love. When grilled, foods reveal their natural flavor; if this is lacking, it can't

be conjured up by magic. And although the philosophy of barbecuing is young and informal, that does not mean it cannot become a matter for real gourmets.

The fire should be lit at least 30 minutes before you start cooking. Learn to master different cooking techniques and manage the heat by trial and error, until you feel comfortable with the "whats", "hows" and "whys" of barbecuing. Never leave the grill unattended, even for a few minutes: try to have everything you need within easy reach, including more charcoal for topping up. It is also important to use different cutting boards and dishes for raw or cooked meat and fish, so as to avoid bacterial contamination.

If you are grilling meat, make incisions along the fatty edges, so as to prevent it from curling while cooking; do not pierce or cut it while it is cooking, as it would lose the juices that keep it tasty and tender. To turn meat, do not use forks, but barbecue tongs or spatulas. Since salt draws the juices out of meat, it is better to add it only a few minutes before removing the food from the grill, with the exception of poultry, which should be salted at the start to make it more savory. Once cooked, do not cut the meat right away: let it stand for a few minutes, so that the inner juices distribute evenly and it remains tender.

Beef is certainly the most appropriate meat for grilling, while veal is perhaps the least suitable (with the exception of chops) because it remains dry and stringy. Lean pork may also be tough, stringy and flavorless when cooked. Ribs and sausages, on the other hand, are perfect.

Fatty fish, such as salmon, mackerel or swordfish, are best for grilling. When roasting whole fish on the barbecue, it is best to make incisions along the side (this allows the heat to penetrate evenly) and to cook them on double-sided easy-turn grates.

The grate must be red hot before placing food on it. Then, once a thin crust has formed on the surface of the food, the temperature should be reduced to prevent burning. After use, grates and skewers should be thoroughly cleaned and degreased, both for reasons of hygiene and to ensure better results at the next barbecue.

Neither fish nor fowl

Who said that barbecues are all about pork chops or roasted prawns? Not only can you grill almost anything, starting with bread (remember the classic Tuscan bruschetta?), but there are also many recipes that are based on neither fish nor fowl, and yet are bursting with flavor. A nice tray of grilled cheeses, vegetables or fruits can be really appetizing.

Soft cheeses are left to melt on slices of grilled bread or polenta, while hard, stringy cheeses, such as tomino, smoked scamorza, caciocavallo or provolone, can be grilled directly on the grate. Once they are ready (they should be removed from the heat before they start to drip), they can be enjoyed straight or flavored with fresh herbs, spices, nuts or dried fruits. Or again, they can be served with picked fruits, honey, jams and sauces, for example pesto.

As regards vegetables, these all lend themselves to grilling. Furthermore, they all – asparagus, eggplant, artichokes, tomatoes, peppers, onions, fennel, zucchini, carrots, leeks, potatoes, pumpkins, red chicory, corn, porcini mushrooms – acquire more flavor and a greater hint of sweetness due to the evaporation of water and the caramelization of sugars during cooking. When grilling vegetables, it is important to know how to control the temperature, to avoid charring them on the outside while being undercooked on the inside. The ideal situation would be to cook the various types of vegetables separately, in similar sized chunk, in double-sided grates.

Grilling fruit is a delicious way of enhancing its aroma, and creating a dessert with pleasantly sweet and sour notes. The ideal fruits for grilling – cut into halves, quarters or thickish slices – are pineapples, oranges, grapefruits, peaches, mangos, papayas, apples, pears, melons, bananas, kiwis, strawberries and apricots. They can be served straight or sprinkled with brown sugar, cinnamon or grated ginger, as well as chopped pistachios, mint leaves or ice cream scoops. The possibilities are endless, and all equally delicious.

An all Italian spirit

The fun culture of barbecuing originated in the United States, but quickly took root in Italy, where it has become a must, from north to south. This is not just because it dips into the country's extraordinary culinary history, filled with delicious grilling recipes since the Middle Ages, but also because it fits perfectly with the traditionally convivial spirit of its people. At a barbecue there is almost never just one cook. Everyone, hosts and guests alike, contributes to the success of the meal. What's more, cooking becomes a time of conviviality, when guests can chat freely with one another.

Academia Barilla, an international center dedicated to the dissemination of Italian gastronomic culture, has selected 50 delicious ways of grilling meat, fish, cheese, vegetables and fruit. Some recipes are classics, such as Italian-style grilled fish, lamb cutlets "a scottadito", grilled peppers, tomino cheese and pineapple. Others, such as the scallop and dried apricot kebab, are original and unusual recipes that, with a touch of imagination, can lead to the creation of truly special dishes.

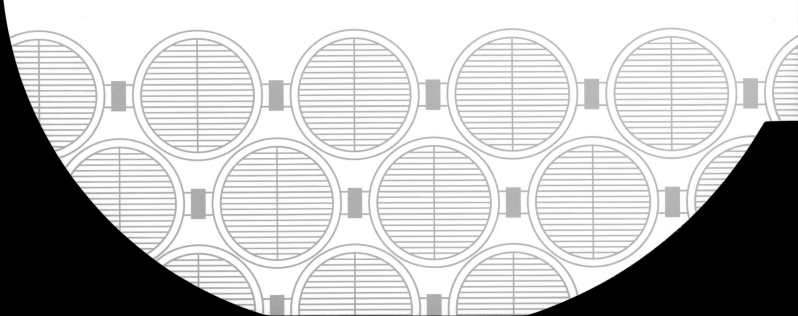

MEAT

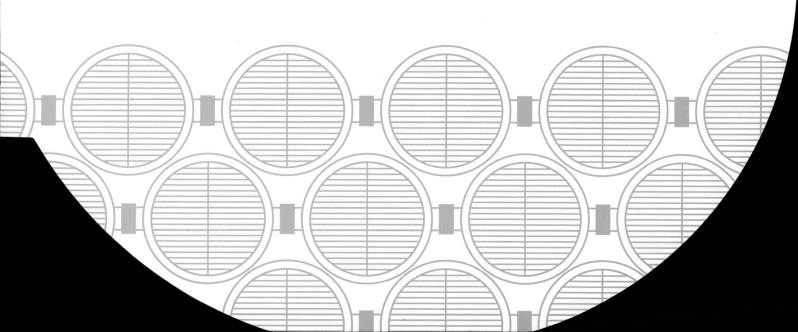

ABRUZZO-STYLE LAMB KEBABS

4 SERVINGS

1 3/4 lb. (800 g) lamb
2 garlic cloves
2 sprigs thyme
2 sprigs rosemary
3 tbsp. plus 1 tsp. (50 ml) extra-virgin olive oil
Salt and pepper
4 wooden skewers

PREPARATION

Cut the meat into cubes of roughly 0.5 in. (1-2 cm), then skewer them.
Wash, dry and pick the thyme and rosemary, then thinly slice the garlic.
Sprinkle the flavorings on the skewers and drizzle with oil.
Let the meat marinate for at least 20-30 minutes in the refrigerator.
To prevent the garlic and thyme from burning while cooking, remove them from the meat before grilling.
Leave the skewers at room temperature for about 10 minutes, and then cook on the grill or griddle
(this will take about 10 minutes). Season with salt and pepper to taste.

Preparation time: 20' - Marinating time: 20-30' - Cooking time: 10'
Difficulty: easy

T-BONE
STEAK

4 SERVINGS

2 T-bone steaks (at least 2 lbs. or 900 g each)
Extra-virgin olive oil (preferably Tuscan)
Salt and pepper
Oil to grease the grill

PREPARATION

Take the T-bone steaks (a cut that includes both short loin and tenderloin) out of the refrigerator
about 30 minutes before cooking, so as to bring them to room temperature.
Place them on a lightly greased hot grill without any seasoning and cook them for 5-7 minutes
per side for medium, or adjust the time depending on how you like your meat. Add salt after cooking.
Let the steaks rest for 5 minutes before serving so that the juices distribute evenly within the meat.
Serve to taste with a sprinkling of freshly ground pepper
and a drizzle of extra-virgin olive oil, preferably Tuscan.

Preparation time: 5' - Cooking time: 10-14'
Difficulty: easy

PORK CHOPS WITH FRESH TOMATOES

4 SERVINGS

4 pork chops (5 oz. or 150 g each)
14 oz. (400 g) ripe tomatoes
3 tbsp. plus 1 tsp. (50 ml) extra-virgin olive oil
2 garlic cloves
1 sprig rosemary
2 sprigs thyme
4 basil leaves
Salt and pepper
Oil to grease the grill

PREPARATION

Wash, seed and dice the tomatoes.
Put them in a glass or steel container and season with salt and pepper, then add a clove of garlic
(peeled and crushed), half the oil and the coarsely chopped basil.
Leave to marinate in the refrigerator for an hour.
Put the chops in a glass or steel container with the remaining oil, rosemary and thyme
and the other garlic clove, either crushed or sliced, for about an hour.
After marinating, cook the chops on a clean, greased grill for 6-7 minutes, then add salt and pepper.
Transfer the cooked chops onto plates and garnish with the tomatoes, after removing the garlic clove.

Preparation time: 20' - Marinating time: 1 h - Cooking time: 6-7'
Difficulty: easy

MINT-MARINATED
LAMB CHOPS

4 SERVINGS

1 1/3 lb. (600 g) lamb chops
1/3 cup plus 2 tbsp. (100 ml) extra-virgin olive oil
1 tbsp. plus 1 tsp. (20 ml) white wine vinegar
1 bunch mint
1 garlic clove
Salt and pepper
Oil to grease the grill

PREPARATION

Wash and dry the mint, then roughly chop two thirds.
Peel and slice the garlic.
In a glass or steel container, mix the vinegar with olive oil, chopped mint and garlic.
If necessary, trim the excess fat from the chops, flatten them slightly,
then marinate them for at least 3 hours in the refrigerator.
Drain the marinade off the chops and cook them on a clean, greased grill for 4-5 minutes per side.
Season with salt and pepper. Serve immediately with a few leaves of fresh mint.

Preparation time: 20' - Marinating time: 3 h - Cooking time: 8-10'
Difficulty: easy

CLASSIC BURGER

4 SERVINGS

1 3/4 lb. (800 g) beef shoulder and/or brisket
1/4 oz. (10 g) butter for the buns
4 hamburger buns
4 lettuce leaves
1 tomato
Ketchup, mayonnaise and mustard
Salt and pepper
Oil to grease the grill

PREPARATION

Use meat that is not too lean, with a fat content of 15-20%.
Run the beef twice through a meat grinder set on a coarse grind.
Divide it into four parts and form the burgers without handling the meat excessively.
Wash and dry the lettuce, then wash the tomatoes and cut them into slices.
Place the burgers on a lightly greased hot grill, then sprinkle with salt and pepper.
Bake for 3-5 minutes per side for medium, or adjust the time depending on how you like your meat.
Season again with salt and pepper after you have turned them over.
Let the burgers rest for 5 minutes before serving so that the juices distribute evenly within the meat.
Meanwhile, cut the buns open, lightly toast the inside on the grill, and then butter them slightly.
Cover the bottom half of each bun with a leaf of lettuce.
Top with the burger, a slice of tomato, and the top half of the bun.
Serve with sauces to taste.

Preparation time: 15' - Cooking time: 6-10'
Difficulty: easy

PORK RIBS
MARINATED IN BEER

4 SERVINGS

2 1/4 lbs. (1 kg) pork ribs (in one piece)
2 3/4 cups (660 ml) beer
3 tbsp. plus 1 tsp. (50 ml) extra-virgin olive oil
1 garlic clove
1 sprig thyme
1 sprig rosemary
Salt and black pepper
Oil to grease the grill

PREPARATION

Remove the hard cuticle on the bone side of the pork ribs.
Peel and chop the garlic together with the thyme and rosemary (washed and dried).
Salt and pepper the ribs and sprinkle with the chopped herbs and garlic.
Briefly massage the herbs over the meat, then place it in a glass or steel container,
and drizzle it with beer (reserve some marinade before adding the meat).
Leave the ribs to marinate in the refrigerator for 12 hours.
Drain the marinade off the meat and cook on very low heat on the clean, greased grill
for about an hour, basting occasionally with some of the reserved marinade.
The meat is cooked when it starts to separate from the bone.
Separate the meat by cutting between the ribs, and serve.

Preparation time: 20' - Marinating time: 12 h - Cooking time: 1 h
Difficulty: easy

VEAL RIBS WITH
FRESH VEGETABLE SAUCE

4 SERVINGS

3 lb. 5 oz. (1.5 kg) veal ribs (in one piece)
3 tbsp. plus 1 tsp. (50 ml) extra-virgin
olive oil
Salt and black pepper

For the sauce
7 oz. (200 g) bell peppers
7 oz. (200 g) tomatoes
3 1/2 oz. (100 g) onions

1 tbsp. chopped parsley
1 garlic clove
1 sprig rosemary
1/3 cup plus 2 tbsp. (100 ml)
extra-virgin olive oil
1 tbsp. plus 1 tsp. (20 ml)
white wine vinegar
1 chili pepper
Salt

PREPARATION

Remove the hard cuticle on the bone side of the veal ribs.
Season with salt and pepper, baste with oil and leave to marinate in the refrigerator for 12 hours.
For the sauce: wash, dry, pick and chop the rosemary;
chop the chili pepper, removing the seeds if you do not want the sauce to be too spicy;
peel and chop the garlic; wash, trim and dice the peppers very finely;
seed and dice the tomatoes finely, then peel and cut the onion in the same way;
put all the ingredients in a bowl with the parsley, vinegar, oil and a pinch of salt
(reserve some marinade before adding the meat), then leave to flavor for at least a couple of hours.
Cook the ribs on very low heat on the clean, greased grill for about 2 hours,
basting occasionally with some of the reserved marinade.
The meat is cooked when it starts to separate from the bone.
Separate the meat by cutting between the ribs, and serve with the fresh sauce.

Preparation time: 20' - Marinating time: 2 h - Cooking time: 2 h
Difficulty: easy

LAMB CUTLETS
"A SCOTTADITO"

4 SERVINGS

1 1/3 lb. (600 g) lamb cutlets
3 tbsp. plus 1 tsp. (50 ml) extra-virgin olive oil
1 sprig thyme
1 sprig rosemary
Salt and pepper

PREPARATION

If necessary, trim the excess fat off the cutlets and flatten them slightly,
then marinate them in a glass or steel container, for 10 minutes
with the extra-virgin olive oil, thyme and rosemary (washed and dried).
Cook the lamb cutlets on the grill for 4-5 minutes per side, then season with salt and pepper.
Serve immediately, while still hot, with a nice
fresh salad or some baked potatoes.

DID YOU KNOW THAT...

Lamb cutlets "a scottadito" (from the Italian for "finger burning"), are typical of Lazio, and Rome in particular.
They are so named because they are best eaten just off the heat, and strictly with your hands
(cutlery is forbidden!), making it easy to burn your fingers. This is a traditional Easter recipe, which, like
other dishes typical of this festivity, is prepared with lamb, an animal that symbolizes innocence and docility,
recalling the sacrifice of Christ on the cross and total submission to the Word of God and His will.

Preparation time: 20' - Marinating time: 10' - Cooking time: 8-10'
Difficulty: easy

GRILLED BEEF TENDERLOIN WITH BALSAMIC VINEGAR REDUCTION

4 SERVINGS

1 3/4 lb. (800 g) beef tenderloin
1/3 cup plus 2 tbsp. (100 ml) balsamic vinegar
3/4 tbsp. (10 g) sugar
Salt and pepper
Oil to grease the grill

PREPARATION

Cut the tenderloin into 4 thick slices. Leave them out of the refrigerator (covered with plastic wrap)
for about 30 minutes before cooking, so that they are at room temperature.
On low heat, reduce the balsamic vinegar with the sugar to about half the initial volume.
Cook the beef tenderloins on a clean, greased grill for 1-3 minutes per side for medium, or adjust
the time depending on how you like your meat. Season with salt and pepper when cooked.
Let the tenderloins rest for 5 minutes before serving so that
the juices distribute evenly within the meat and it is easier to cut.
Serve drizzled to taste with the balsamic vinegar reduction.

Preparation time: 20' - Cooking time: 2-6'
Difficulty: easy

COCKERELS MARINATED IN BALSAMIC VINEGAR

4 SERVINGS

2 cockerels (1 lb. 2 oz. or 500 g each)
3 tbsp. plus 1 tsp. (50 ml) balsamic vinegar
1/3 cup plus 2 tbsp. (100 ml) extra-virgin olive oil
2 sprigs thyme
1 sprig sage
1 sprig rosemary
1 bay leaf
Salt and pepper
Oil to grease the grill

PREPARATION

Cut the cockerels in half. Wash and dry.
Flatten slightly, season with salt and pepper, and place in a glass or steel container.
Wash, pick and mince all the herbs, mix them with the balsamic vinegar, and then add the oil.
Pour the mixture onto the cockerels, leaving some aside,
and marinate in the refrigerator for at least an hour.
Drain the marinade off the cockerels and cook on a clean, greased grill.
Brush with the remaining marinade while cooking, turning the cockerels over and brushing
them with the marinade from time to time, for about 30 minutes in all.

Preparation time: 20' - Marinating time: 1 h - Cooking time: 30'
Difficulty: easy

JAMAICA-STYLE PORK

4 SERVINGS

2 1/4 lbs. (1 kg) pork shoulder
5-6 chili peppers (preferably Scotch
Bonnet or Habanero)
2 spring onions
2 shallots
2 garlic cloves
1 tbsp. fresh thyme, picked
2 tsp. black pepper, ground
1 tbsp. ground allspice
2 1/2 tbsp. (30 g) brown sugar

3 1/2 tsp. (20 g) salt
1/3 cup plus 2 tbsp. (100 ml) extra-virgin
olive oil
Juice of 1 lime
1 tsp. cinnamon, ground
1/2 tsp. nutmeg, ground
1 piece ginger
2 oranges
Oil to grease the grill
Orange juice (optional)

PREPARATION

Peel and grate the ginger; wash the chili peppers and slice open to remove the seeds.
Trim the garlic, spring onions and shallots.
Place all the ingredients, except the pork, in the food processor and blend well
until the mixture is fairly liquid (if necessary, dilute with some orange juice).
In a glass or steel container, marinate the pork in the sauce (keeping a little aside) for at least 12 hours.
Drain the marinade off the meat and cook on a clean, lightly greased grill, on medium heat,
basting with the sauce kept aside if the meat should start to dry up.
Cut the meat into thick slices and, if desired, serve with the remaining sauce.

Preparation time: 15' - Marinating time: 12 h - Cooking time: 1 h
Difficulty: easy

GRILLED FRESH BACON

4 SERVINGS

1 3/4 lb. (800 g) fresh pork bacon
3/4 cup plus 5 tsp. (200 ml) red wine
1 garlic clove
1 sprig rosemary
3 sprigs thyme
3 sage leaves
1 bay leaf
4-5 juniper berries
Salt
1 tsp. black peppercorns
Oil to grease the grill

PREPARATION

Wash, dry and coarsely chop the herbs, then peel and slice the garlic.
Using the flat side of a knife blade, crush the berries and peppercorns.
Cut the fresh bacon into roughly 1 in. (2 cm) slices,
season with salt and sprinkle with the chopped herbs and the spices.
Place the meat in a glass or steel container and pour over the wine.
Leave to marinate for at least 3 hours in the refrigerator.
Drain the marinade off the bacon and cook on a clean, greased grill,
on medium heat, for 8-10 minutes per side.

Preparation time: 20' - Marinating time: 3 h - Cooking time: 16-20'
Difficulty: easy

HONEY-GLAZED
DUCK BREAST

4 SERVINGS

2 duck breasts
3 tbsp. (60 g) honey
Salt and pepper
Oil to grease the grill

PREPARATION

Make diamond shaped incisions on the skin of the duck breasts,
after trimming off the excess.
Season the breasts generously with salt and pepper and massage them slightly,
then place them on a clean, greased grill, skin side down.
While cooking, baste with honey using a small brush.
Cook for about 15 minutes, making sure that the breasts remain pink inside.
Let the honey-glazed duck breasts stand wrapped in foil for a few minutes before slicing them.
Serve brushed with a little more honey, if desired.

Preparation time: 20' - Cooking time: 15'
Difficulty: easy

CHICKEN BREAST MARINATED IN GINGER AND CORIANDER

4 SERVINGS

1 1/3 lbs. (600 g) chicken breast without skin
1 cup (250 ml) plain yogurt
1 tbsp. fresh coriander, minced
1 piece ginger
1 garlic clove
Juice of 1 lemon
Salt and pepper
Oil to grease the grill

PREPARATION

Peel and grate the ginger, then peel and chop the garlic.
Place them in a container with the lemon juice,
fresh coriander, salt and pepper, then mix in the yogurt.
Trim and slice the chicken breast into 4 pieces.
Cover the chicken breast with the yogurt and marinate in the refrigerator for at least 4 hours.
Wipe off excess marinade, then cook the chicken on a clean, greased grill for about 10 minutes.

Preparation time: 20' - Marinating time: 4 h - Cooking time: 10'
Difficulty: easy

DEVILED CHICKEN

4 SERVINGS

1 whole chicken, around 2 1/4 lb. (1 kg)
1/4 cup (60 g) mustard
Breadcrumbs, finely ground
Salt and pepper
Cayenne
Oil to grease the grill

PREPARATION

Wash and dry the chicken. Cut the chicken open
along the back, and flatten it. Season generously with salt, pepper and cayenne.
Brush the entire chicken with mustard and roll it in breadcrumbs, making sure that they adhere well.
Cook the deviled chicken on a clean, greased grill for about 35 minutes.

DID YOU KNOW THAT...

There are two possible theories on why this chicken recipe is called "deviled" (or, "alla diavola" in Italian).
According to some, hell and the devil are evoked by the flames on which the chicken is cooked;
for others, it is an allusion to the recipe's use of cayenne, a particularly spicy
chili pepper native to the city of Cayenne, in French Guiana, which symbolically
evokes the "strong sensations" that one might feel in Hades.

Preparation time: 20' - Cooking time: 35'
Difficulty: easy

GRILLED VEAL BRISKET

4 SERVINGS

4 1/2 lbs. (2 kg) veal brisket (boneless)
3 tbsp. plus 1 tsp. (50 ml) extra-virgin olive oil
1 tsp. peppercorns
2 sprigs rosemary
2 sprigs thyme

2 sprigs Santoreggia herb (savory)
1 tsp. oregano
2 bay leaves
1 sprig sage
1 tsp. juniper berries
Coarse salt
Oil to grease the grill

PREPARATION

Pick and chop all the herbs, then crush the peppercorns
and juniper berries with the flat side of a knife blade.
Grease the meat with oil, then marinate it with the herbs and spices
for about 3 hours in a glass or steel container.
Once marinated, place the veal brisket on a clean,
greased grill and cook on very low heat. Cover the grill, if possible.
Salt the meat generously with coarse salt (it will only absorb the amount needed).
After about an hour, turn the meat over and grease it with a little oil if necessary.
After about a couple of hours, when the brisket is cooked,
wrap it in foil and let it rest for at least 15 minutes
so that the juices distribute evenly within the meat and it is easier to cut.

Preparation time: 30' - Marinating time: 3 h - Cooking time: 2 h
Difficulty: easy

LAMB KEBABS MARINATED IN GINGER, YOGURT AND INDIAN SPICES

4 SERVINGS

1 lb. 2 oz. (500 g) lean lamb shoulder
1 cup (250 ml) plain yogurt
1 tbsp. garam masala
1 piece ginger
Salt
Oil to grease the grill
4 wooden skewers
naan (optional)

PREPARATION

Peel and grate the ginger, then put it in a container with the yogurt and add the *masala* spices.
Trim the excess fat off the lamb shoulder and cut the meat into roughly 1 in. (3 cm) chunks.
Leave the meat to marinate with the yogurt and spices in the refrigerator for at least 4 hours.
Drain the marinade off the lamb then skewer the meat chunks.
Cook on a clean, greased grill for about 15 minutes, then season with salt.
If desired, serve on a bed of naan, a mideastern flatbread.

Preparation time: 20' - Marinating time: 4 h - Cooking time: 15'
Difficulty: easy

MARINATED CHICKEN AND SPRING ONION KEBAB

4 SERVINGS

4 chicken thighs
4 tbsp. (60 ml) white wine
1 tbsp. plus 2 tsp. (25 ml) extra-virgin olive oil
1 tbsp. (15 ml) soy sauce
4 spring onions
Salt and pepper
Oil to grease the grill
4 wooden skewers, about 5 in. (12 cm) long

PREPARATION

Remove the skin from the chicken, then cut the meat into roughly 1 in. (2 cm) cubes.
Leave it to marinate in a glass or steel container with the soy sauce,
white wine and olive oil for about 2 hours, reserving some marinade before adding the chicken.
Meanwhile, trim and wash the fresh spring onions and cut them into 1-1.5 in. (3-4 cm) chunks.
Once marinated prepare the skewers, alternating the chicken and spring onions,
and then cook for about 10 minutes on a clean, greased grill. Season with salt and pepper.
While cooking, baste with some of the reserved marinade using a small brush.

Preparation time: 30' - Marinating time: 2 h - Cooking time: 10'
Difficulty: easy

TURKEY AND SAGE KEBAB
WITH POLENTA

4 SERVINGS

14 oz. (400 g) turkey loin
3 tbsp. plus 2 tsp. (50 ml) extra-virgin olive oil
1 bunch sage
2 cups (500 ml) water
3/4 cup (100 g) cornmeal for instant polenta
Salt and pepper
Oil to grease the grill
4 wooden skewers

PREPARATION

Prepare the polenta, sprinkling the cornmeal slowly into the boiling salted water.
Cook for about 5 minutes, stirring often with a wooden spoon.
Pour the polenta into a baking pan and let cool.
When it is cold, cut it into cubes of about 1 in. (2 cm) per side.
Cut the turkey loin into cubes of size equal to those of the polenta.
Leave the meat to marinate in a glass or steel container for at least 30 minutes,
with the oil and a few sage leaves (washed and dried), then prepare the skewers,
alternating the turkey chunks with a sage leaf and a cube of polenta.
Cook the skewers on a clean, greased grill. Season with salt and pepper to taste.

Preparation time: 60' - Marinating time: 30' - Cooking time: 10'
Difficulty: easy

MIXED ITALIAN-STYLE KEBAB

4 SERVINGS

2 chicken thighs
5 oz. (150 g) lean beef
5 oz. (150 g) lean pork
(or fresh bacon)
5 oz. (150 g) fresh
sausage links
1 onion
1 bell pepper

1 sprig rosemary
2 sprigs thyme
2 bay leaves
3 tbsp. plus 1 tsp. (50 ml)
extra-virgin olive oil
Salt and pepper
Oil to grease the grill
4 wooden skewers

PREPARATION

Remove the skin from the chicken. Cut the chicken, beef and pork into roughly 1 in. (3 cm) cubes.
Cut the sausage into chunks. Let the meat (except the sausage) marinate for a few hours
in separate glass or steel containers, with the herbs, olive oil and freshly ground pepper.
Meanwhile, trim and wash the bell pepper and peel the onion.
Cut the pepper into roughly 1 in. (3 cm) squares and the onion into strips of similar size.
Prepare the skewers, alternating the meats with pieces of pepper and onion.
Cook them on a clean, greased grill for about 10 minutes, then season with salt.

Preparation time: 35' - Marinating time: 2 h - Cooking time: 10'
Difficulty: easy

SLICED BEEF WITH ARUGULA, PARMIGIANO REGGIANO AND TRADITIONAL BALSAMIC VINEGAR

4 SERVINGS

2 slices beef short loin (about 12 1/2-14 oz. or 350-400 g each)
3 1/2 oz. (100 g) arugula
3 1/2 oz. (100 g) Parmigiano Reggiano cheese
1 sprig rosemary
1 sprig thyme
1 bay leaf
Traditional Balsamic Vinegar
Extra-virgin olive oil
Salt and pepper
Oil to grease the grill

PREPARATION

Place the beef in a glass or steel container and leave to marinate
with the herbs and olive oil in the refrigerator for 1 1/2 hours.
Meanwhile, wash and thoroughly dry the arugula and shave the
Parmigiano Reggiano using a cheese slicer (or a vegetable peeler).
Remove the meat from the refrigerator about 30 minutes before cooking, so that it is at room temperature.
Drain the marinade off the meat and cook on a clean, lightly greased grill for 3-5 minutes per side
for medium, or adjust the time depending on how you like your meat. Season with salt and pepper.
Let the short loin stand for 5 minutes, so that the juices distribute evenly within the meat, then cut into
roughly 1 in. (2 cm) slices. Arrange them on a plate, garnished with arugula and Parmigiano Reggiano shavings.
Add a drizzle of extra-virgin olive oil and a few drops of Traditional Balsamic Vinegar.

Preparation time: 15' - Marinating and resting time: approx. 2 h - Cooking time: 6-10'
Difficulty: easy

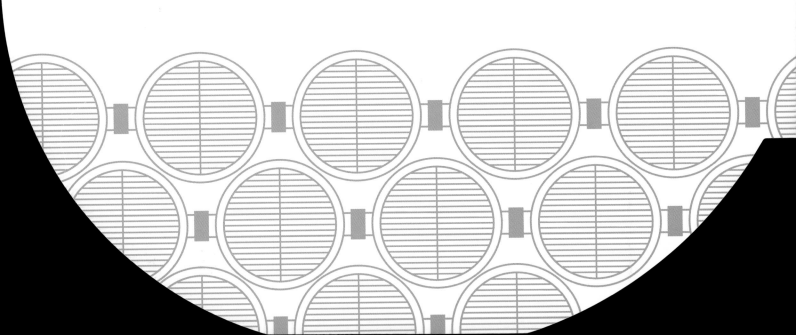

FISH

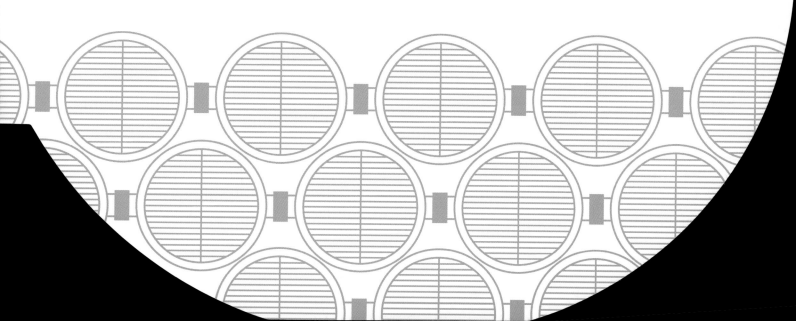

PEPPER-CRUSTED TUNA STEAK

4 SERVINGS

1 3/4 lb. (800 g) tuna steak
3 tbsp. plus 1 tsp. (50 ml) extra-virgin olive oil
2 oz. (60 g) black peppercorns
2 lemons
Salt

PREPARATION

Coarsely crush the peppercorns using the flat side of a knife blade or a meat tenderizer.
Cut the tuna steak into thick slices, grease lightly and roll in pepper, pressing slightly so it adheres well.
Brush the tuna steaks with the remaining oil and cook on the grill for 2-3 minutes
per side for medium, or adjust the time depending on how you like your fish. Add salt to taste.
Serve the pepper-crusted tuna steaks with lemon wedges.

DID YOU KNOW THAT...

The term "tuna" refers to a genus of the Scombridae family, which includes eight
large predatory fish. The most commonly sold tunas are the *Thunnus albacares*, known
as the "yellowfin tuna", a particularly widespread oceanic species, and the *Thunnus thynnus*,
known as the "bluefin tuna", characteristic of the Mediterranean Sea and now an endangered species.
From a nutritional standpoint, there are significant differences between these two fishes:
the flesh of the bluefin tuna has more calories because it contains more fat,
but it is also rich in healthy Omega-3 fatty acids and phosphorus.

Preparation time: 15' - Cooking time: 4-6'
Difficulty: easy

MARINATED AND GRILLED
THAI-STYLE SHRIMP

4 SERVINGS

20 shrimp
2 lemongrass stalks
1 piece ginger
1 garlic clove
4 basil leaves (preferably Thai)
2 tsp. (10 ml) soy sauce
1 tbsp. plus 1 tsp. (20 ml) extra-virgin olive oil
1 tsp. green curry paste
1-2 chili peppers
Salt and pepper
Oil to grease the grill
4 wooden skewers

PREPARATION

Peel and grate the ginger; peel and chop the garlic; cut the basil (preferably Thai) into strips;
slice the lemongrass and 1 or 2 chili peppers to taste.
Put them all in a container with the soy sauce, a pinch of salt and pepper, the green curry paste and the oil.
Peel the shrimp, keeping the tails.
Devein the shrimp and marinate them with the other ingredients for at least a couple of hours.
Drain off the marinade and skewer the shrimp, then cook them on a clean, greased grill for 4-5 minutes.
Pull them off the skewers before serving.

Preparation time: 30' - Marinating time: 2 h - Cooking time: 4-5'
Difficulty: easy

GRILLED PRAWNS WRAPPED IN BACON WITH A DRIZZLE OF TRADITIONAL BALSAMIC VINEGAR

4 SERVINGS

12 prawns
12 slices pancetta
Traditional Balsamic Vinegar
Salt and pepper
Oil to grease the grill

PREPARATION

Peel the prawns, keeping the heads and tails, then devein.
Season the prawns with a pinch of salt and pepper, then wrap the tail of each
with a slice of pancetta. Cook on a clean, greased grill for about 4-5 minutes,
then serve with a drizzle of Traditional Balsamic Vinegar.

DID YOU KNOW THAT...

Traditional Balsamic Vinegar, made from cooked grape must, left to ferment and acetify
and then aged for at least 12 years, is typical of the cuisine of Modena and Reggio Emilia,
and would appear to date back to Roman times.
What's certain, is that this delicious condiment became known and appreciated outside the local boundaries
as a refined product suited to the tables of the European aristocracy during the golden age
of Modena, under the rule of the powerful Este family, Lords of Ferrara.
Centuries later, Traditional Balsamic Vinegar still retains this noble trait.

Preparation time: 20' - Cooking time: 4-5'
Difficulty: easy

ITALIAN-STYLE GRILLED FISH

4 SERVINGS

4 squid
4 soles, small
4 scallops
8 sardines
4 prawns
4 slices swordfish (about 2 3/4 oz. or 80 g each)
1/3 cup plus 2 tbsp. (100 ml) extra-virgin olive oil
1/2 garlic clove, minced
1 tbsp. parsley, minced
3 1/2 oz. (100 g) breadcrumbs
2 lemons
Salt and pepper
Oil to grease the grill

PREPARATION

Clean, scale and wash all the fish. Clean and wash the shellfish.
Mix the breadcrumbs with the garlic and minced parsley.
Salt and pepper the ingredients, then grease them lightly with olive oil
and roll them in the flavored breadcrumbs, ensuring they adhere well.
Cook all the ingredients on a clean, greased grill.
Serve with lemon wedges.

Preparation time: 30' - Cooking time: 15'
Difficulty: easy

WARM SQUID SALAD WITH ROSEMARY OIL

4 SERVINGS

8 squid, small
3 tbsp. plus 1 tsp. (50 ml) extra-virgin olive oil
2 sprigs rosemary
3 1/2 oz. (100 g) mixed salad
A drizzle of balsamic vinegar
Salt and pepper

PREPARATION

Pick the rosemary leaves and infuse for about an hour in half the oil,
heated to a temperature of about 140 °F (60 °C).
Clean and wash the squid thoroughly.
Grease lightly with extra-virgin olive oil, then grill on both sides and season with salt and pepper.
Season the salad with olive oil and balsamic vinegar and arrange some on each plate.
Slice the squid, arrange them on the plates and serve drizzled with the rosemary oil.

Preparation time: 1 h - Cooking time: 8'
Difficulty: easy

GRILLED SEA BREAM
ON VINE LEAVES

4 SERVINGS

4 sea bream (around 10.5 oz. or 300 g each)
4 tbsp. (60 ml) extra-virgin olive oil
2 garlic cloves
4 sprigs thyme
16 vine leaves
Juice of 1 lemon
Salt and pepper
Oil to grease the grill

PREPARATION

Clean, scale and wash the sea bream.
Sprinkle some salt and pepper inside each fish, then add a sprig of thyme and half a clove of garlic.
Salt and grease the outside of the fish with a little oil.
Place 2 slightly overlapping vine leaves on a clean, greased grill and place a sea bream on top.
Repeat with all the fish.
Halfway through cooking, after about 8-10 minutes, flip the fish over and place it on new vine leaves.
While the fish is cooking, mix the remaining oil with the lemon juice.
Serve the grilled fish with the oil and lemon juice dressing.

Preparation time: 15' - Cooking time: 16-20'
Difficulty: easy

HERB-MARINATED SEA BREAM WITH GRILLED PRAWNS

4 SERVINGS

4 sea bream (around 10.5 oz. or 300 g each)
12 prawns
1/3 cup plus 2 tbsp. (100 ml) extra-virgin olive oil
4 sprigs thyme
4 sprigs fresh marjoram
1 tsp. oregano

2 sprigs tarragon
1 bunch parsley
1 bunch coriander
Juice of 1 lemon
1 garlic clove, minced
Salt and pepper
Oil to grease the grill

PREPARATION

Clean, scale, wash and fillet the sea bream.
Arrange the fillets in a glass or steel container and sprinkle with the chopped garlic
and with a third of the herbs, previously trimmed, washed, dried and picked.
Drizzle with a little olive oil and leave to marinate for about 2 hours.
Peel the prawns and marinate these separately, using a marinade as for the sea bream.
Once marinated, place the lightly salted and peppered sea bream fillets
on a clean, greased grill, then also grill the prawns.
While the fish is cooking, mix the remaining oil with the lemon juice and the remaining minced herbs.
When cooked, serve the prawns on the sea bream, drizzled with the oil and lemon juice dressing.

Preparation time: 15' - Marinating time: 2 h - Cooking time: 10'
Difficulty: easy

SWORDFISH IN SALMORIGLIO SAUCE

4 SERVINGS

1 1/3 lbs. (600 g) swordfish fillet
Juice of 2 lemons
1 garlic clove
1 tbsp. parsley, minced
1 tsp. oregano
3/4 cup plus 1 tbsp. (200 ml) extra-virgin olive oil
3 tbsp. plus 1 tsp. (50 ml) water
Salt and pepper

PREPARATION

Cut the swordfish fillet into 4 slices.
For the Salmoriglio sauce, place the oil in a bowl and add the lemon juice
and hot water, then beat with a whisk.
Add the garlic, the minced parsley and the oregano, then emulsify the sauce in a double boiler,
beating with a whisk for 5-6 minutes.
Grease the fish slices with a little of the Salmoriglio sauce and cook on a griddle or grill for 5 minutes,
basting with a dash of sauce while cooking.
Season with salt and pepper.
Serve the slices of swordfish drizzled with more Salmoriglio sauce.

Preparation time: 15' - Cooking time: 5'
Difficulty: easy

GRILLED OCTOPUS
WITH CITRUS AND FENNEL

4 SERVINGS

1 lb. 2 oz. (500 g) octopus
1 onion
1 carrot
1 celery stalk
1 fennel
1 orange
1 grapefruit

2 3/4 oz. (80 g) black olives, pitted
4 tbsp. (60 ml) extra-virgin
olive oil
Salt and pepper
Black pepper
Oil to grease the grill
Wild fennel (optional)

PREPARATION

Peel the carrot and the onion, then trim the celery and cut the vegetables into chunks.
Bring a pot of salted water to the boil, then add the vegetables. Cook for 5 minutes, then add the octopus.
Cook for about 40 minutes or until the octopus is tender when pierced with a knife.
Wash and clean the fennel, slice it very finely and soak it in cold water to prevent it from darkening.
Peel the orange and grapefruit and remove the white pith.
Cut the orange into segments to be added to the salad, removing the membrane.
Repeat with the grapefruit, then with your hands squeeze the juice of the remaining citrus fruit into a bowl.
Add salt, pepper and 5 tablespoons of olive oil to the juice.
Mix with a whisk to obtain a dressing for the salad.
When you have drained the octopus, remove the tentacles and cook on a clean, greased grill.
Meanwhile, prepare the salad on a serving platter: arrange the drained and dried fennel,
the orange and grapefruit segments, and the pitted black olives. Add the grilled octopus and season
with the dressing, a sprinkling of ground black pepper and, if desired, a few bunches of wild fennel.

78

Preparation time: 1 h - Cooking time: 10'
Difficulty: easy

GRILLED SALMON WITH
BELL PEPPER SAUCE

4 SERVINGS

1 1/2 lb. (700 g) salmon fillet
1 red pepper, firm and fleshy
4 slices Parma ham
Fennel seeds
Vegetable broth
Salt and pepper
Oil to grease the grill

PREPARATION

Wash the pepper and cook on a clean, greased grill,
flipping it over when the skin begins to scorch.
As soon as it is cooked (it should be soft but not mushy), remove from the grill
and place in a tightly closed food bag (the steam will make it easier to peel).
Peel and seed the pepper, then blend it with some vegetable broth flavoured with a pinch of salt.
Skin the salmon and cut it into 4 slices, then add a pinch of salt and pepper.
Sprinkle the slices of salmon with some fennel seeds and wrap them in ham.
Cook on a clean, greased grill for about 10 minutes,
Serve with the pepper sauce.

Preparation time: 45' - Cooking time: 10'
Difficulty: easy

GRILLED SALMON WITH DILL SAUCE

4 SERVINGS

4 slices of salmon (about 5 1/2 oz. or 160 g each)
1 tsp. mustard
1 tsp. (5 ml) wine vinegar
1/4 cup (100 g) mayonnaise
1 bunch dill
Extra-virgin olive oil
Salt and pepper
Oil to grease the grill

PREPARATION
Wash, dry and chop the dill coarsely.
Mix the mustard with the vinegar, then add the dill and mayonnaise.
If the sauce is too thick, dilute it with a tablespoon of warm water.
Grease the salmon steaks with olive oil and cook on a clean,
greased grill for about 8 minutes overall. Season with salt and pepper.
Serve with the dill sauce.

Preparation time: 15' - Cooking time: 8'
Difficulty: easy

SPICED SALMON
WITH LIME AND CHILI SAUCE

4 SERVINGS

1 3/4 lb. (800 g) salmon fillet
1 tsp. fennel seeds
1 tsp. coriander seeds
1/2 tsp. cumin seeds
1 piece ginger
1 tbsp. plus 1 tsp. (20 ml)
extra-virgin olive oil
Salt and pepper

Oil to grease the grill
1/2 red onion
2 spicy chili peppers
1 ripe tomato, large
Juice of 2 lime
1 tbsp. plus 1 tsp. (20 ml)
extra-virgin olive oil
1 tbsp. fresh coriander, minced

PREPARATION

Pound the cumin, fennel and coriander seeds and the ginger (peeled and grated)
in a mortar or mince them not too finely in the *food processor*.
Grease the salmon fillet with extra-virgin olive oil, then sprinkle
the skinless side with the spices, a pinch of salt and freshly ground pepper.
Cut into 4 slices, leaving the skin, then cook on a clean, greased grill.
For the sauce, peel the onion, seed the peppers and tomatoes, and squeeze the lime.
Cut the ingredients coarsely, then chop them not too finely in the blender.
Add the oil and the minced fresh coriander, and stir. Serve with the chili sauce on the side.

Preparation time: 40' - Cooking time: 10'
Difficulty: easy

GRILLED MACKEREL
WITH MEDITERRANEAN VEGETABLES

4 SERVINGS

1 3/4 lb. (800 g) mackerel
8 3/4 oz. (250 g) eggplant
7 oz. (200 g) zucchini
7 oz. (200 g) yellow bell pepper
7 oz. (200 g) red bell pepper
5 1/2 oz. (160 g) carrots
5 oz. (150 g) red Tropea onions
4 oz. (120 g) vine tomatoes
Basil
1/3 cup plus 2 tbsp. (100 ml) extra-virgin olive oil
Salt and pepper

PREPARATION

Trim, wash and slice the eggplant, carrots and zucchini.
Cut the tomato and onions into slices.
Grill the sliced vegetables and whole peppers (after which you should peel and cut them into strips)
and then, in a baking dish, marinate them for at least an hour with olive oil,
a pinch of salt and coarsely chopped basil.
Clean, wash and dry the mackerel, sprinkle the inside with salt and pepper,
then grease them lightly with oil. Grill on both sides over medium heat for about 25 minutes overall.
Serve hot with the marinated vegetables.

Preparation time: 1 h 30' - Marinating time: 1 h - Cooking time: 25'
Difficulty: easy

SCALLOP AND DRIED APRICOT KEBAB

4 SERVINGS

12 scallops
8 dried apricots
1 tbsp. plus 2 tsp. (25 ml) extra-virgin olive oil
Juice of 2 oranges
1 chili pepper
Salt
Oil to grease the grill
4 wooden skewers

PREPARATION

Squeeze the oranges and emulsify the juice with the oil, salt and sliced chili pepper,
then marinate the scallops for about an hour, keeping some marimade aside.
If very dry, rehydrated the apricots by placing them in water for about 10 minutes.
Prepare the skewers, alternating the scallops and apricots.
Cook for about 10 minutes on a clean, greased grill.
While cooking, baste with the remaining marinade using a small brush.

Preparation time: 30' - Marinating time: 1 h - Cooking time: 10'
Difficulty: easy

SESAME TUNA KEBAB

4 SERVINGS

1 lb. 2 oz. (500 g) tuna steak
1/3 cup (50 g) sesame seeds
2 1/2 tbsp. (50 g) acacia honey
Salt and pepper
Oil to grease the grill
4 wooden skewers

PREPARATION

Cut the tuna steak into roughly 1 in. (3 cm) chunks, then skewer them.
Salt and pepper the tuna, then brush it lightly with honey.
Roll the tuna skewers in the sesame seeds, ensuring they adhere well.
Cook the sesame tuna skewers on a clean, greased grill for about 4-6 minutes.

DID YOU KNOW THAT...

The tiny sesame seeds, used in the kitchen not only as breading, as in this recipe,
but also as condiment or in the dough of breads, crackers and bread sticks,
enclose a whole host of valuable nutrients. In addition to having a high calcium content,
ranging from 800 to 1000 mg per 3.5 oz. (100 g) of product, they also contain
phosphorus, magnesium, iron, manganese, zinc and selenium.
It is from the incredible properties of these seeds, providing vitality
and strength, that the magic formula "Open Sesame" is supposed to derive.

Preparation time: 15' - Cooking time: 4-6'
Difficulty: easy

GRILLED TUNA STEAK
WITH LEMON AND CAPERS

4 SERVINGS

1 1/3 lb. (600 g) tuna steak
1 oz. (25 g) capers preserved in salt
2 lemons
3 tbsp. plus 1 tsp. (50 ml) extra-virgin olive oil
Salt and pepper
Oil to grease the grill

PREPARATION

Cut the tuna steak into 4 slices
and marinate for a few minutes with a drizzle of extra-virgin olive oil.
Meanwhile, peel one of the 2 lemons, removing the pith and the membrane between the segments
with a sharp knife, then dice the pulp, making sure to keep the juice.
Desalt the capers by placing them in water for 5 minutes.
Squeeze the second lemon and emulsify the juice with oil, salt and pepper.
Season both sides of the tuna fillets with salt and pepper to taste
and arrange them on a grill lightly greased with oil, then cook as desired.
Serve the tuna sprinkled with the diced lemon and capers, and drizzled with the lemon and oil dressing.

Preparation time: 20' - Cooking time: 4-5'
Difficulty: easy

GRILLED TROUT
WITH LEMON, SAGE
AND EXTRA-VIRGIN OLIVE OIL

4 SERVINGS

4 trouts (7 oz. or 200 g each)
2 lemons
8 sage leaves
3 tbsp. plus 1 tsp. (50 ml) extra-virgin olive oil
Salt and pepper

PREPARATION

Wash and dry the sage, then wash, dry and thinly slice the lemons.
Clean, wash and dry the trouts. Salt and pepper the inside,
season with a dash of extra-virgin olive oil, and insert
two sage leaves and two or three slices of lemon into each trout.
Grease the outside of the fish with the remaining oil and cook on a clean grill for about 15 minutes.

DID YOU KNOW THAT...

Common sage (scientific name: *Salvia officinalis*), a herb originating in the Mediterranean,
has been used in the kitchen since antiquity to flavor mainly meats and fish,
but also pastas, soups and cheeses.
Sage is also very much used in herbal medicine for its extraordinary healing properties.
Not surprisingly, its Latin name confirms its reputation: the name *Salvia* derives from the
Latin verb *salvere* ("to feel well and healthy"), the verb related to *salus*, meaning "health".

Preparation time: 15' - Cooking time: 15'
Difficulty: easy

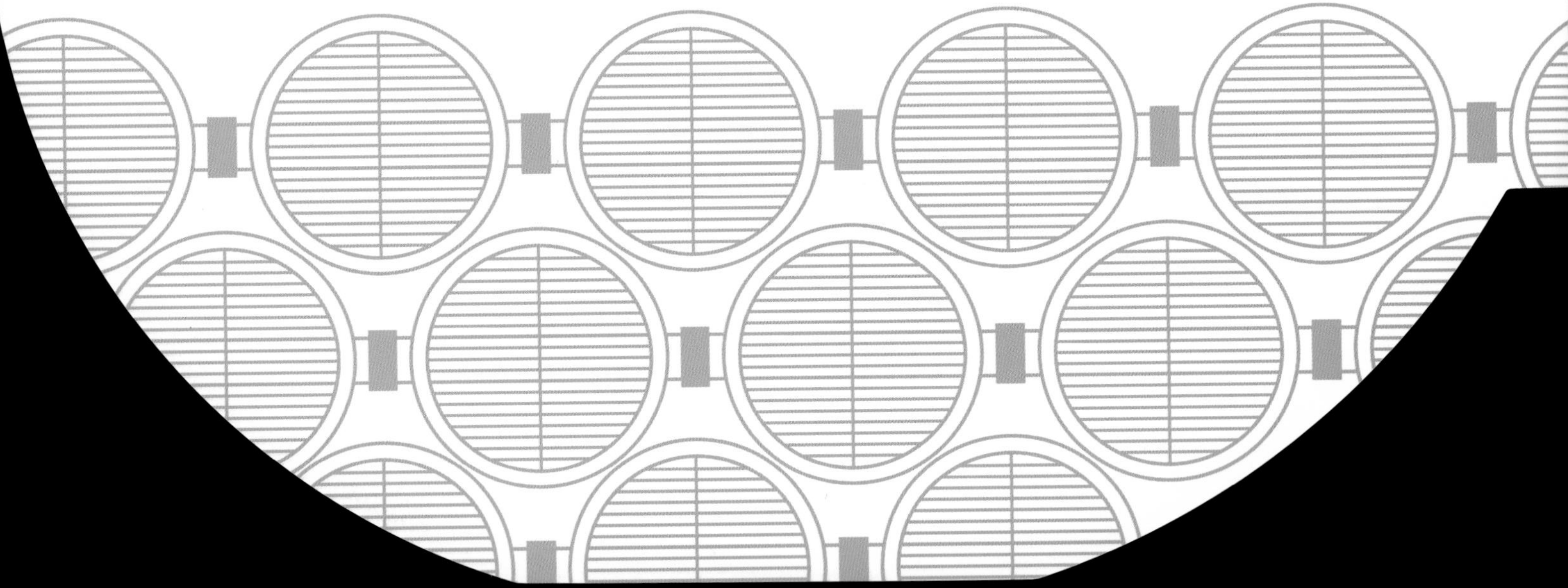

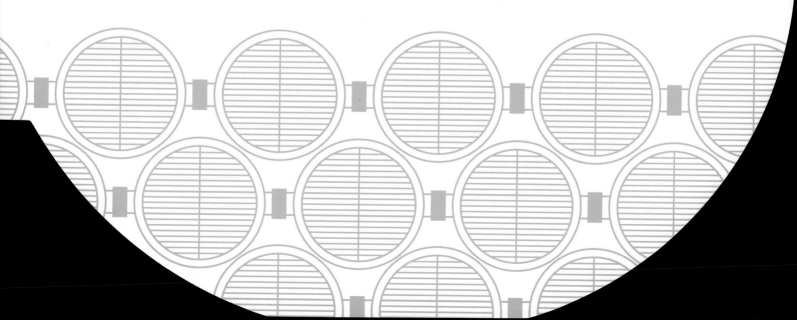

FRUIT AND VEGETABLE DISHES

97

GRILLED PINEAPPLE WITH BROWN SUGAR AND RUM

4 SERVINGS

1 pineapple
1/4 cup (50 g) brown sugar
3 tbsp. plus 1 tsp. (50 ml) rum

PREPARATION

Peel the pineapple carefully and remove the central core using a special corer.
Cut the pineapple into thickish slices and leave it to marinate with the rum for about 15 minutes.
Drain the slices, pat them dry with kitchen paper, then sprinkle a pinch of brown sugar
and place them on a thoroughly cleaned grill.
When they are caramelized, turn them over and cook on the other side.
While cooking, brush the pineapple with the marinade.
It can be served warm or cold, accompanied, if desired, with a scoop of ice cream.

Preparation time: 10' - Marinating time: 15' - Cooking time: 30'
Difficulty: easy

GARLIC BRUSCHETTA
WITH EXTRA-VIRGIN OLIVE OIL,
TOMATO AND BASIL

4 SERVINGS

14 oz. (400 g) bread (loaf)
10 1/2 oz. (300 g) plum tomatoes
2 tbsp. (30 ml) extra-virgin olive oil
4 basil leaves
2 garlic cloves
Salt
Oil to grease the grill

PREPARATION

Cut the bread into 0.5 in. (1 cm) thick slices and toast on an oiled grill.
Once the bruschettas are toasted, peel a garlic clove and use it to rub half of the slices
either lightly or abundantly, according to your taste. Drizzle these with a little olive oil
(use half the dose indicated in the recipe) and sprinkle with a pinch of salt.
Dice the tomatoes and season them with salt, the other half of the oil, the second garlic clove
(crushed, or chopped for a stronger taste) and the coarsely chopped basil.
Leave to flavor for a few minutes.
Just before serving, sprinkle the tomatoes on the remaining toasted slices of bread.

Preparation time: 20' - Cooking time: 5'
Difficulty: easy

GRILLED PORCINI MUSHROOM CAPS

4 SERVINGS

4 Porcini mushroom caps
1/2 garlic clove, minced
1 tbsp. parsley, minced
1 1/2 tbsp. (20 g) butter
2 tsp. (10 ml) extra-virgin olive oil
Salt
Oil to grease the grill

PREPARATION

Carefully clean the mushroom caps with a damp cloth.
Grease them with extra-virgin olive oil and place them on a clean, greased grill, stem side down.
Flip them over after a couple of minutes, then season with salt.
Sprinkle with the minced garlic and parsley, and place a knob of butter in the center of each.
Cover the grill, if possible, and finish cooking.

Preparation time: 10' - Cooking time: 5'
Difficulty: easy

GRILLED CROSTINI
WITH CHERRY TOMATOES AND OLIVES

4 SERVINGS

7 oz. (200 g) bread (*baguette*)
7 oz. (200 g) cherry tomatoes
2 tbsp. (30 ml) extra-virgin olive oil
8 3/4 oz. (250 g) buffalo mozzarella
1 oz. (30 g) Taggiasca olives, pitted
Oregano
Salt
Oil to grease the grill

PREPARATION

Wash the cherry tomatoes and cut them in half. Cut the mozzarella into strips.
Cut the bread into 4 sections and cut each section in half (as if you were to make a sandwich).
Toast the bread on a greased grill, cut side down.
Remove the bread from the grill and lay the tomatoes on the toasted side of each crostini,
then season with a pinch of salt and a sprinkling of oregano.
Add the mozzarella and olives, then put the crostini back on the grill and cover it, if possible.
Serve with a drizzle of extra-virgin olive oil.

Preparation time: 20' - Cooking time: 5'
Difficulty: easy

GRILLED CORN
ON THE COB

4 SERVINGS

4 corn cobs, fresh or vacuum-sealed
2 tbsp. (30 g) butter
Salt and pepper
Oil to grease the grill

PREPARATION

Clean the cobs and rinse them well in water.
If they still have the husks, wrap these around the cobs and cook on a clean, greased grill.
After about 10 minutes, remove the husks and continue cooking for another 10 minutes,
brushing the cobs with melted butter and a pinch of salt and pepper.
Turn them often. If you are using pre-cooked, vacuum-sealed corn cobs,
reduce the cooking time by half and brush them with the melted butter from the beginning.

Preparation time: 10' - Cooking time: 10-20'
Difficulty: easy

GRILLED POTATOES
STUFFED WITH CHEESE

4 SERVINGS

4 potatoes, medium
5 oz. (150) g cheese of your choice
1 1/2 tbsp. (20 g) butter
Salt and pepper

PREPARATION

Wash the potatoes with their skins, wrap them individually in foil and cook
on the grill over medium heat for about 30 minutes, depending on the size.
As soon as they are cooked, cut them in half and empty them slightly with a spoon.
Arrange a piece of cheese (such as Provola) in the center of each, then put the two halves back together,
wrap the potatoes up again and put them on the grill for another 5 minutes.
Open the foil and serve the potatoes with a knob of butter,
a pinch of salt and a sprinkle of freshly ground pepper.

Preparation time: 10' - Cooking time: 35'
Difficulty: easy

GRILLED BELL PEPPERS
WITH GARLIC, ANCHOVIES
AND EXTRA-VIRGIN OLIVE OIL

4 SERVINGS

2 bell peppers, large, firm and fleshy
1 garlic clove
4 salted anchovies or 8 anchovy fillets in oil
1 tbsp. parsley, minced
1 tbsp. plus 2 tsp. (25 ml) extra-virgin olive oil
Oregano
Salt
Oil to grease the grill

PREPARATION

Wash the peppers and cook them on a clean, greased grill, turning them over when the skin begins to scorch.
As soon as they are cooked (they should be soft but not mushy),
remove them from the grill and place them in a tightly closed food bag
(the steam will make them easier to peel).
When cool, skin and seed the peppers, then cut them into 4 strips each
and season them with a pinch of salt. Place an anchovy fillet, 1-2 slices of garlic
and a pinch of chopped parsley and oregano on each strip.
Finish off with a drizzle of extra-virgin olive oil.

Preparation time: 1 h - Cooking time: 20'
Difficulty: easy

GRILLED POLENTA WITH GORGONZOLA CHEESE

4 SERVINGS

2 cups (500 ml) water
2/3 cup (100 g) cornmeal for instant polenta
7 oz. (200 g) Gorgonzola cheese
Salt
Oil to grease the grill

PREPARATION

Prepare the polenta, sprinkling the cornmeal slowly into the boiling salted water.
Cook for about 5 minutes, stirring often with a wooden spoon.
Pour the polenta into a baking pan and let cool.
When it is cold, cut it into cubes of about 0.5-1 in. (1.5-2 cm) per side.
Brown the slices of polenta lightly on a clean, greased grill,
then turn them over and place a piece of Gorgonzola on each.
Serve when the cheese begins to melt.

Preparation time: 20' - Cooking time: 6'
Difficulty: easy

STUFFED DRIED PLUMS, WRAPPED IN BACON AND GRILLED

4 SERVINGS

12 dried plums
2 oz. (60 g) Caprino goat's cheese
6 slices pancetta
Oil to grease the grill
4 wooden skewers

PREPARATION

Stuff each plum with a piece of goat's cheese
and wrap it in half a slice of pancetta.
Skewer the stuffed plums three at a time on each wooden skewer
and cook on a clean, greased grill for about 5 minutes.

DID YOU KNOW THAT...

While fresh plums contain antioxidant substances and are a good source
of vitamin C, potassium, copper, manganese, carotenoids and vitamins K and B6,
dried plums have an even higher concentration of nutrients.
They are an effective tonic with significant purifying and energizing properties,
making them particularly suitable for sportmen. They also boast the added benefit of being free of saturated
fat and added sugars, as well as promoting a sense of fullness after a meal due to the presence of fibers.

Preparation time: 20' - Cooking time: 5'
Difficulty: easy

GRILLED FRUIT
KEBAB

4 SERVINGS

1/2 pineapple
2 peaches
2 bananas
4 apricots
1 3/4 oz. (50 g) coconut, grated
1 tbsp. (20 g) honey or maple syrup
Oil to grease the grill
4 wooden skewers

PREPARATION

Wash and cut the peaches in half, without peeling them.
Take out the stone and cut each peach half into 4 pieces.
Wash and pit the apricots.
Peel the pineapple carefully, removing the central core using a special corer,
and cut it into thick slices.
Peel and chop the bananas into chunks.
Alternate the various types of fruit on the wooden skewers.
Place the skewers on a clean, greased grill, turning them on all sides as they cook.
When they are ready, arrange them on a plate, drizzle them with honey or maple syrup,
and roll them in grated coconut.

Preparation time: 20' - Cooking time: 7-8'
Difficulty: easy

VEGETARIAN KEBAB

4 SERVINGS

2 zucchini
8 whitebutton mushrooms
8 cherry peppers
8 cherry tomatoes
1 red onion
6 basil leaves
1/3 cup plus 2 tbsp. (100 ml) extra-virgin olive oil
Salt and pepper
Oil to grease the grill
4 wooden skewers

PREPARATION

Wash the zucchini and cut them into slices about 3 in. thick.
Wash the basil, blanch it in salted water, then cool it immediately in iced water.
Drain and blend it with extra-virgin olive oil.
Clean the peppers, removing the stem and seeds, then wash them. Wash the tomatoes.
Peel the onion and cut it into slices similar in size to the other ingredients.
Clean and wash the mushrooms.
Prepare the skewers, alternating the various ingredients.
Cook the vegetarian kebabs on a clean, greased grill, turning them on all sides as they cook.
Serve with a pinch of salt and pepper and a drizzle of basil-flavored olive oil.

Preparation time: 30' - Cooking time: 7-8'
Difficulty: easy

GRILLED TOMINO CHEESE
WITH SMOKED BACON

4 SERVINGS

4 tomino cheese wheels
8 slices smoked bacon
4 slices rustic bread
1 tbsp. plus 1 tsp. (20 ml) extra-virgin olive oil
Oil to grease the grill

PREPARATION

Wrap each tomino wheel in two slices of smoked bacon, arranging them perpendicularly to one another.
Place the cheese on a clean, greased grill and cook for 1-2 minutes per side.
They will be ready when the bacon is golden and the cheese begins to melt.
Serve with slices of bread drizzled with extra-virgin olive oil and toasted for one minute per side.

DID YOU KNOW THAT...

Tomino is a typical cheese from Piedmont. Small and cylindrical in shape,
it can be produced entirely from goat's milk, or from a mixture of cow's and goat's milk.
The dough of the fresh cheese is white and soft, and the taste is slightly acidic.
The ripened cheese has a thin rind and a yellow dough,
and when heated, gives off a stronger, more persistent odor.

Preparation time: 5' - Cooking time: 2-4'
Difficulty: easy

ALPHABETICAL INDEX OF RECIPES

123

ALPHABETICAL INDEX
OF INGREDIENTS

All the photographs are by Academia Barilla except

©123RF: immagine timer; Igor Dutina/Shutterstock: page 8; Floortje/iStockphoto: page 5;
Lapina Maria/Shutterstock: page 14; Ockra/iStockphoto: page 128; Lauri Patter/iStockphoto:
page 11; svry/Shutterstock: page 13; TheCrimsor/iStockphoto: pages 7, 122, 123;
Volosina/Shutterstock: page 126; Sergiy Zavgorodny/Shutterstock: page 2

ACADEMIA BARILLA

AMBASSADOR OF ITALIAN CUISINE IN THE WORLD

In the heart of Parma, recognized as one of the most prestigious capitals of cuisine, the Barilla Center stands in the middle of Barilla's historical headquarters, now hosting Academia Barilla's modern structure. Founded in 2004 with the aim of affirming the role of Italian culinary arts, protecting the regional gastronomic heritage, defending it from imitations and counterfeits and to valorize the great tradition of Italian cooking, Academia Barilla is where great professionalism and unique competences in the world of cuisine meet. The institution organizes cooking courses for those passionate about food culture, offering services dedicated to the operators in the sector and proposing products of unparalleled quality. Academia Barilla was awarded the "Business-Culture Prize" for its promotional activities regarding gastronomic culture and Italian creativity in the world. Our headquarters were designed to meet the educational needs in the field of food preparation and has the multimedia tools necessary to host large events: around an extraordinary gastronomic auditorium, there is an internal restaurant, a multisensory laboratory and various classrooms equipped with the most modern technology. In our Gastronomic Library we conserve over 11,000 volumes regarding specific topics and an unusual collection of historical menus and printed materials on the culinary arts: the library's enormous cultural heritage is available online and allows anyone to access hundreds of digitalized historical texts. This forward thinking organization and the presence of an internationally renowned team of professors guarantee a wide rage of courses, able to satisfy the needs of both catering professionals as well as simple cuisine enthusiasts. Academia Barilla also organizes cultural events and initiatives for highlighting culinary sciences open to the public, with the participation of experts, chefs and food critics. It also promotes the "Cinema Award", especially for short-length films dedicated to Italian food traditions.

www.academiabarilla.it

WHITE STAR PUBLISHERS

WS White Star Publishers® is a registered trademark
property of De Agostini Libri S.p.A.

© 2014 De Agostini Libri S.p.A.
Via G. da Verrazano, 15
28100 Novara, Italy
www.whitestar.it - www.deagostini.it

Translation: Soget s.r.l.

ISBN 978-88-544-0825-8
2 3 4 5 6   18 17 16 15 14

Printed in China

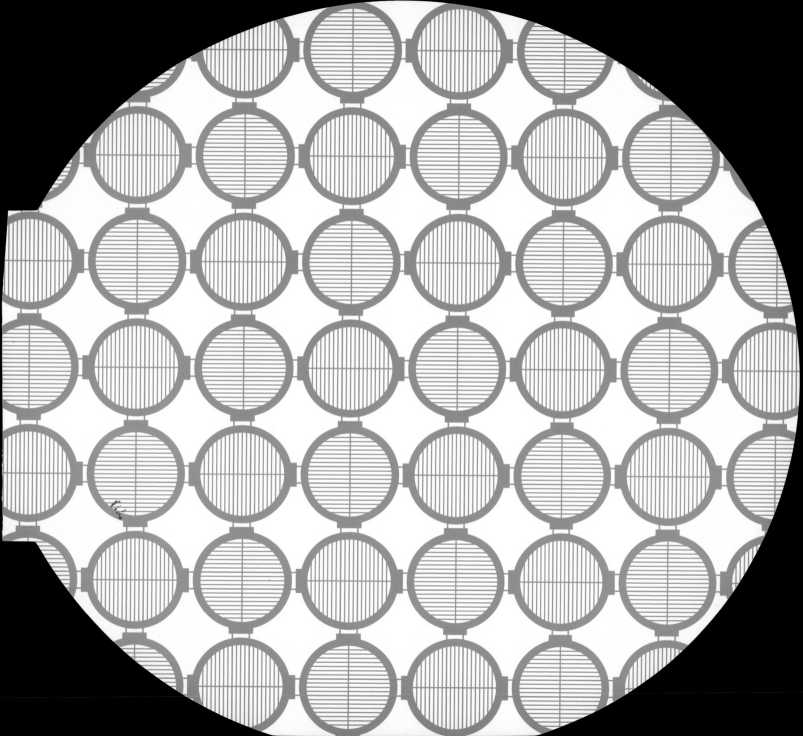

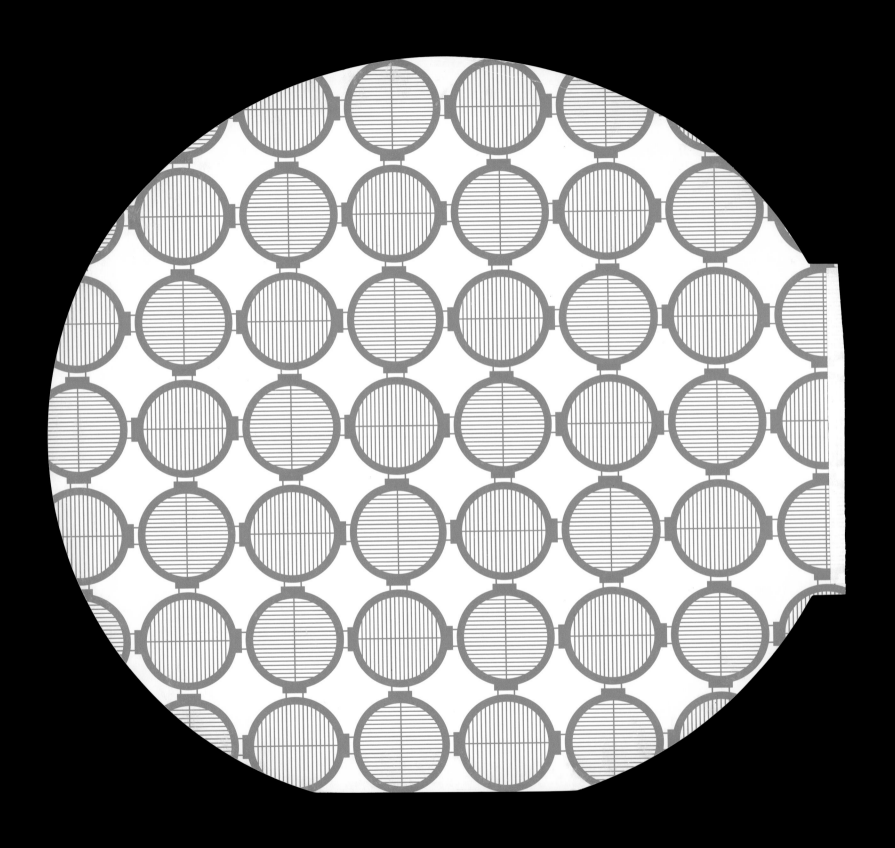